THE
NEW YORKER
BOOK OF MONEY CARTOONS

BLOOMBERG PRESS

PRINCETON

THE NEW YORKER
BOOK OF MONEY CARTOONS

THE INFLUENCE, POWER, AND OCCASIONAL INSANITY
OF MONEY IN ALL OF OUR LIVES

EDITED BY ROBERT MANKOFF
INTRODUCTION BY CHRISTOPHER BUCKLEY

PUBLISHED BY BLOOMBERG PRESS

First edition published 1999

3 5 7 9 10 8 6 4 2

The New Yorker book of money cartoons : the influence, power, and
    occasional insanity of money in all of our lives / edited by Robert
    Mankoff; introduction by Christopher Buckley. -- 1st ed.
        p.   cm.
    Includes index.
    ISBN 1-57660-033-5 (alk. paper)
        1. Money--Caricatures and cartoons. 2. American wit and humor,
    Pictorial. 3. New Yorker (New York, N.Y.: 1925)   I. Mankoff,
    Robert. II. New Yorker (New York, N.Y.: 1925)
    NC1428.N47   1999a
    741.5'973--dc21   99-36941
                                                              CIP

Book design by LAURIE LOHNE / **Design It Communications**

THE
NEW YORKER
BOOK OF MONEY CARTOONS

BY CHRISTOPHER BUCKLEY

ATTENTION!

Halfway Through This Introduction You Will Find a List of Bill Gates' Ten Favorite Stocks!

Not really. Just a shameless attempt to get your attention. Writing an introduction to any collection of *New Yorker* cartoons is enough to make even the most self-confident person feel like a speed bump outside the entrance to the Grand Prix. But in the event one, just one of you—perhaps you're a slow page turner, perhaps a stockroom clerk at the bookstore spilled honey and your fingers stuck here on the way to the first cartoon—is reading this, then, please, don't skip ahead. Read on, if only so that you can say afterwards, "You know, I love these books of *New Yorker* cartoons, but why the heck do they waste time putting introductions in them?"

One of the first Latin quotations any schoolchild of my generation was given to translate, and meditate upon, was the old Chaucer chestnut "*Radix malorum est cupiditas* (The love of money is the root of all evil)." The sentiment sounded okay back in the fifth grade. Now that I have a fifth grader of my own, I would translate it differently: "The love of money is the root of all tuition." It would be silly, not to say downright dumb, standing as we are at the threshold of a book of *New Yorker* cartoons on the subject, to strike any high-minded pose. Let's be honest: the love of money is the root of *everything*.

Money has certainly always been the root of humor at the magazine that, since 1925, has published 60,000 cartoons. In the beginning, its founding editor, Harold Ross, scraped together a meager operating budget, which provided the staff with a working environment that could not be called lavish. None of them ever called it that. The late Brendan Gill, an aboriginal *New Yorker* staffer, used to regale listeners with a hilarious description of how he had to walk over the desks of three other staffers in order to reach his own. One day Ross demanded of Dorothy Parker why she had not handed in the article that was due. She replied, "Someone was using the pencil."

The root of all evil continued to be the root of a lot of mirth among the *New Yorker's* legendary staff. After James Thurber's short story "The Secret Life of Walter Mitty" was turned into a big box office movie success starring Danny Kaye, Samuel Goldwyn tried to hire Thurber away from the magazine to be one of his contract writers at the studio. Goldwyn offered him $500 a week, a salary that in 1947 would have weakened the knees of most *New Yorker*—or for that matter, New York—writers. But Thurber cabled back that "Mr. Ross has met the increase."

Goldwyn knew Hollywood, but he seems not to have known Harold Ross, who no more would have paid a writer $500 a week than he would have bought another pencil for him. The movie mogul thereupon offered Thurber $1,000 a week. Thurber wired back again that Mr. Ross had met the increase. Goldwyn upped his offer to $1,500. Again, Thurber replied with an identical cable. Finally Goldwyn offered $2,500 (that's $18,972.60 in today's dollars). Still Thurber wouldn't budge.

Eventually Goldwyn lost interest and stopped his importuning. But then, sometime later, he renewed his siren song, this time offering Thurber $1,500, apparently forgetting his previous offer of $2,500.

"I'm sorry," Thurber cabled back, "but Mr. Ross has met the decrease."

Twentieth-century literature and culture are better off for Thurber's (remarkable) resistance, but a number of *New Yorker* staffers did succumb to the lure of Hollywood. When one of them, John McNulty, headed west, Ross's valedictory comment to him consisted of, "Well, God bless you, McNulty, goddamn it."

According to Robert Mankoff, who as cartoon editor of *The New Yorker* assembled—and himself contributed to—this collection, of the 13,000 cartoons that the magazine has run since 1986, one-quarter of them have been on the subject(s) of business and money. Most *New Yorker* cartoonists, he points out wryly, have never gotten near business.

Have they gotten "near" money?

"Not near enough!"

This obdurate reality no doubt accounts for their tone of ironic detachment.

Twenty-five percent seems like a lot, when you consider the other available themes, such as, well, let's see, love, death…lawyers, cats? But Mr. Mankoff explains that, until fairly recently (1992, with the arrival of Tina Brown as editor), *The New Yorker*'s cartoons never touched one of life's major themes. (Sex. Shhhhh…) He attributes the cartoonists' obsession with business and money as a "sublimation" of this forbidden territory. One grasps his point. If you can't have sex, you might as well make do with money. It's pretty reliable.

"I'm tired of Love: I'm still more tired of Rhyme, But money gives me pleasure all the time," as Hilaire Belloc put it. Or as Jack Benny, in his signature skit, said to the mugger who had accosted him with, "Your money or your life," and who was now demanding to know what the delay was, "I'm *thinking...*"

The 1980s were about Wall Street's riches. The 1990s have been about the trickle-down money. Your money, my money, the other person's money, most frequently referred to as, "How come he has more money than me?" The decade has been "about" other things, to be sure: the Internet and e-mail, cell phones, IPOs, Microsoft, Amazon.com, and so many other things that go dot.com in the night that you'd need a Pentium Processor just to keep track of them all. But one way or the other, all these miscellaneous marvels have one thing in common. As the singer in *Cabaret* would say: "Money, money, money, money, money" (not to be too reductionist).

According to *The Wall Street Journal*, over the last five years, U.S. households have created $13 trillion of net new wealth. If that strikes you as a lot, or even as a ton of dough, as Federal Reserve Chairman Alan Greenspan would put it, you are in fact correct. Thirteen trillion dollars equals the entire U.S. bond market. Ten years ago the richest person on the Forbes 400 was John Kluge, with a net worth of about $5.2 billion. In 1999 the richest person on the list was—surprise—Bill Gates, with $90 billion. It's been a while since I took Econ 101, but I think this is called exponential growth. One of my favorite *New Yorker* cartoons—collected in the recent *The New Yorker Book of Business Cartoons*—is Jon Agee's pastiche on the National Debt Clock near Times Square in New York City. This one is called "Bill Gates' Wealth." Beneath the lighted main display of continuously increasing, mind-boggling numbers is a subcategory on the debt clock labeled, as in the original, "Your family's contribution." In this collection, we have Mick Stevens' "Your Pizza Dollar," with slices representing the constituent parts: pepperoni, mushrooms, insurance, taxes...all of it your contribution to the pizza man's wealth.

But it's not just that the rich have gotten richer. Everyone has gotten richer. (Okay, except for you and me.) That dorky guy you went to high school with now has his own Gulfstream V airplane. One of the longest-running books on *The New York Times* bestseller list is called *The Millionaire Next Door.* According to its authors, that guy next to you in the supermarket—looking for the best buy in jumbo boxes of generic raisin bran, wearing a ripped, eight-year-old sweater from the Lands' End catalogue and driving a rusty twelve-year-old Corolla—is richer than Croesus!

When I was growing up in the sixties, one of the coolest shows on TV was called *The Millionaire,* about an old moneybucket who gave away a million dollars a pop to people in distress—whose lives were not necessarily improved by the windfall. Just the name of the show alone was exotic and alluring and unattainable. Your parents would whisper of someone, "He's a millionaire." Once upon a time, the rich would cluster in places like *The Great Gatsby*'s East Egg, where "people played polo and were rich together." Now they're next door. They'd no longer all fit in East Egg. Even Seattle must be getting cramped.

In the fifties and sixties, it was considered impolite to ask people how much they made. Now magazines devote entire issues to "Who Made What." I never had the foggiest idea, or really even interest in, how much Walt Disney made from his magic kingdom. But a newspaper recently reported that Disney Chairman Michael Eisner made—good golly—$570 million, so I know now. I could probably even calculate My Family's Contribution. Why didn't I make $570 million last year? Obviously, I need one of Roz Chast's Wonderwallets (see page 2): "I know there's only seven bucks in here—but <u>it looks like seven hundred!</u>" The genius of a *New Yorker* cartoonist is, to paraphrase Emerson, that they know exactly what we're thinking.

This book's timing is perfect, coming at the end of our American millennial, funny, money-mad decade. There's nothing to capture the zeitgeist (German for "wish we had a word like that in English for 'spirit of the times'") as a *New Yorker* cartoon, and the spirit of our era is hilariously recorded here, especially on page 44, in the one by Gahan Wilson showing the prisoner in the bunk above exclaiming cheerfully to the gloomy one in the bunk below, "Well, anyhow, it sure is handy having my broker right here in my cell!" At a time when everything is for sale, Edward Frascino's cartoon pretty much says it all: the tooth fairy hovering over an elderly gent in bed, announcing: "Hi, I'm the tooth fairy. Want to buy back some of your teeth?" We spent a lot of time thinking about health—and "managed"—care in the nineties. Frank Cotham sure nailed that zeitgeist in his cartoon showing the clever doctor outside the intensive care unit consoling the bereaved relative of the deceased: "His final wish was that all his medical bills be paid promptly." And there's a warning, as well as a laugh, in the one on page 77 by Bernard Schoenbaum, showing two world-weary dogs walking along, one saying to the other, "Let's face it—man's best friend is money."

And yet *New Yorker* cartoons at their best, which these are, amount to more than just expressions of a particular period. They're non-ephemeral, timeless. Their wit, joy, and—dare I say it? Yes, what the heck, I do!—truths do not, like milk, expire. They'll probably be as funny in 2099 as they are in 1999. What master of the universe—at any time, in any age—would not enjoy an uneasy giggle at Mick Stevens' cartoon of the man standing before a scowling Saint Peter at the Pearly Gates and being told, "You had more money than God. That's a big no-no." And there's Mort Gerberg's Leonardo da Vinci, interrupting his work-in-progress portrait of a woman with an inscrutable smile to paint an even larger canvas entitled, "Production Expenses: Project—Lisa, Mona." Charles Barsotti shows two oppressed working stiffs staring philosophically at something going on offstage, one saying to the other, "There, there it is again—the invisible hand of the marketplace giving us the finger." That could have run in 1929 or during the last recession.

Finally—piquantly, to-the-pointly—there's the one by Henry Martin of two men strolling down a street where every sign, every ad, every awning, flag, and license plate displays the same word: "Money." One says to the other, "Remember a few years ago when everything was sex, sex, sex?"

Sort of. Or has it always been money, money, money? You could look it up in Chaucer, or you could just settle back and enjoy this timeless, comforting, and wise collection of riches.

"If debt is a measure of consumer confidence, we have become very confident indeed."

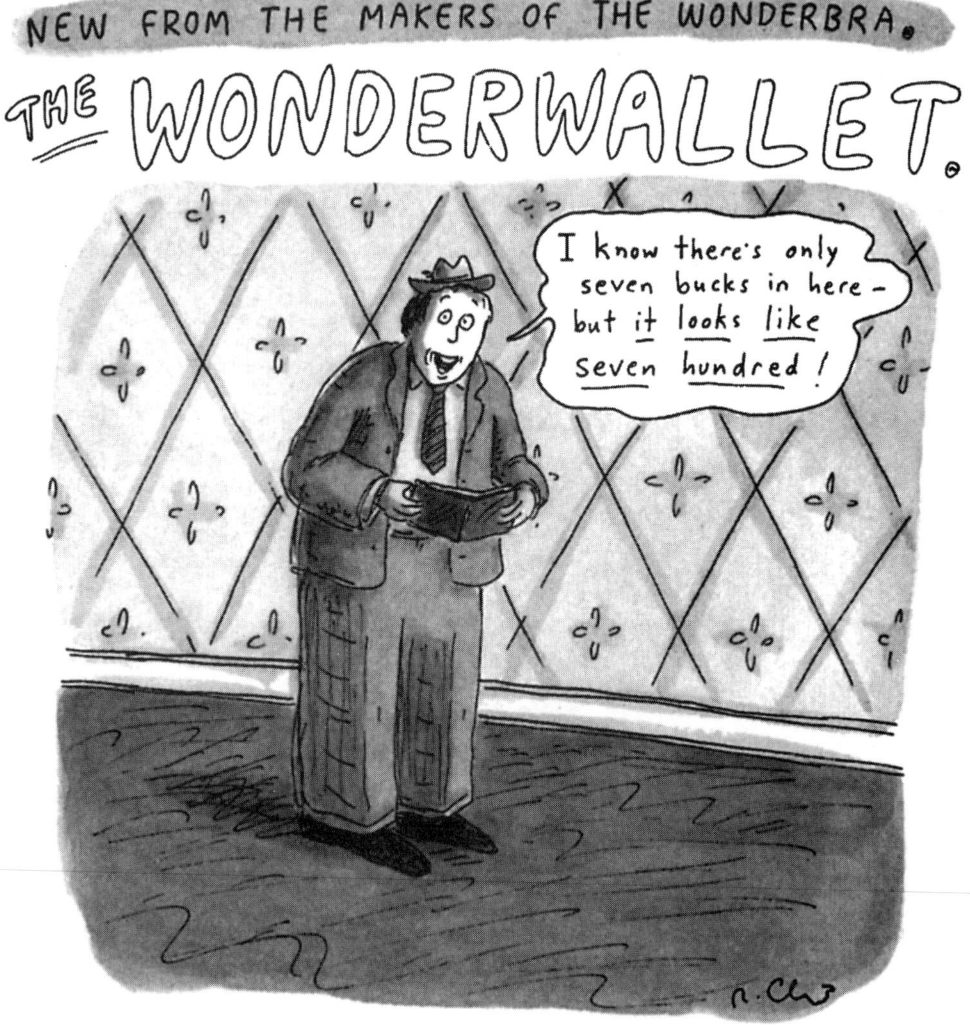
NEW FROM THE MAKERS OF THE WONDERBRA.
THE WONDERWALLET.
I know there's only seven bucks in here - but it looks like seven hundred!

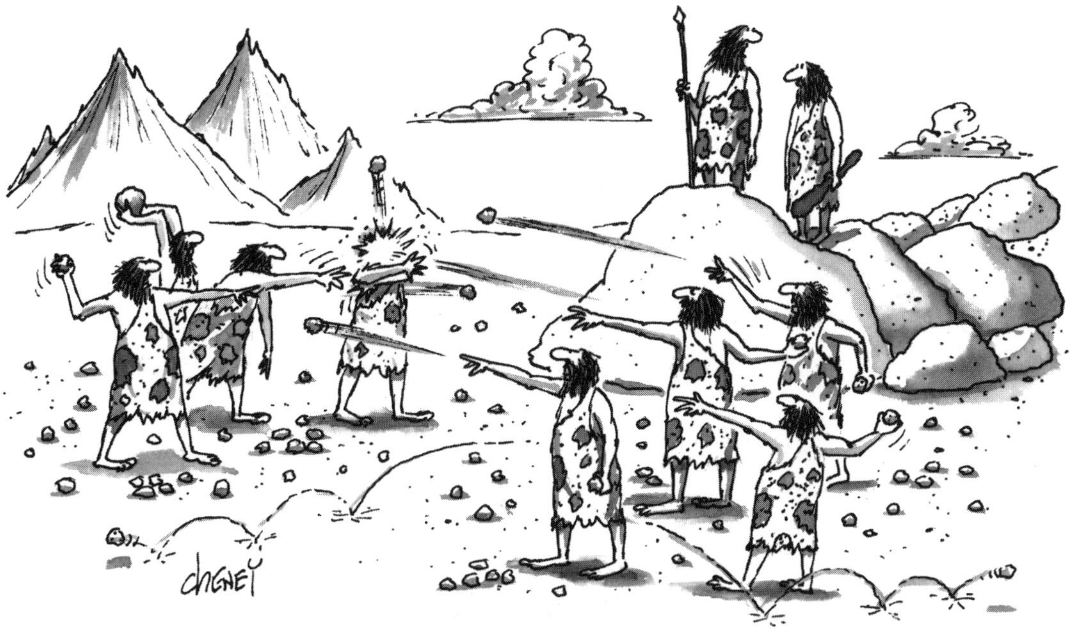
CHENEY

"Trading is heavy today."

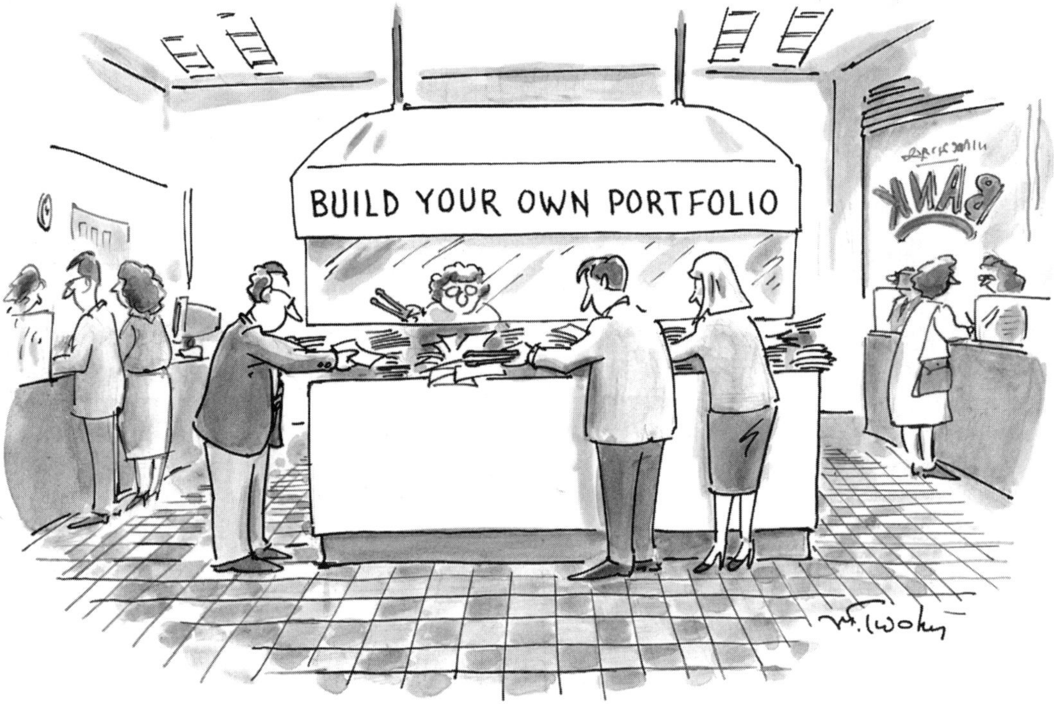
BUILD YOUR OWN PORTFOLIO

"We're buying into the dream of home ownership."

"*I married you for your money, Leonard. Where is it?*"

"Nonsense—I can sit on my Warhols twice as long as you can sit on yours."

"Come on, honey. We may no longer be 'nouveau,' but at least we're still 'riche.'"

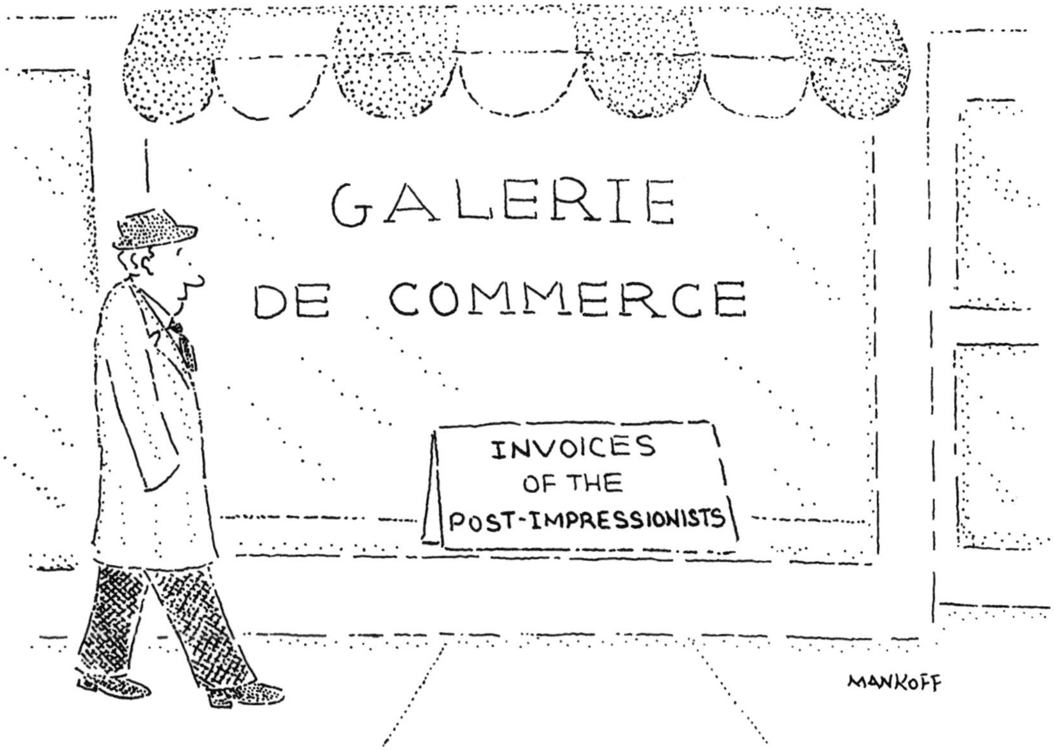
GALERIE
DE COMMERCE
INVOICES
OF THE
POST-IMPRESSIONISTS
MANKOFF

"Quite frankly, I'm a bit disappointed."

"O.K. The forward rate for marks rose in March and April, combined with a sharp increase in German reserves and heavy borrowing in the Eurodollar market, while United States liquid reserves had dropped to fourteen billion dollars, causing speculation that the mark might rise and encouraging conversion on a large scale. Now do you understand?"

"*I hunt and she gathers—otherwise, we couldn't make ends meet.*"

"Welcome aboard. You are now exempt from federal, state, and local taxes."

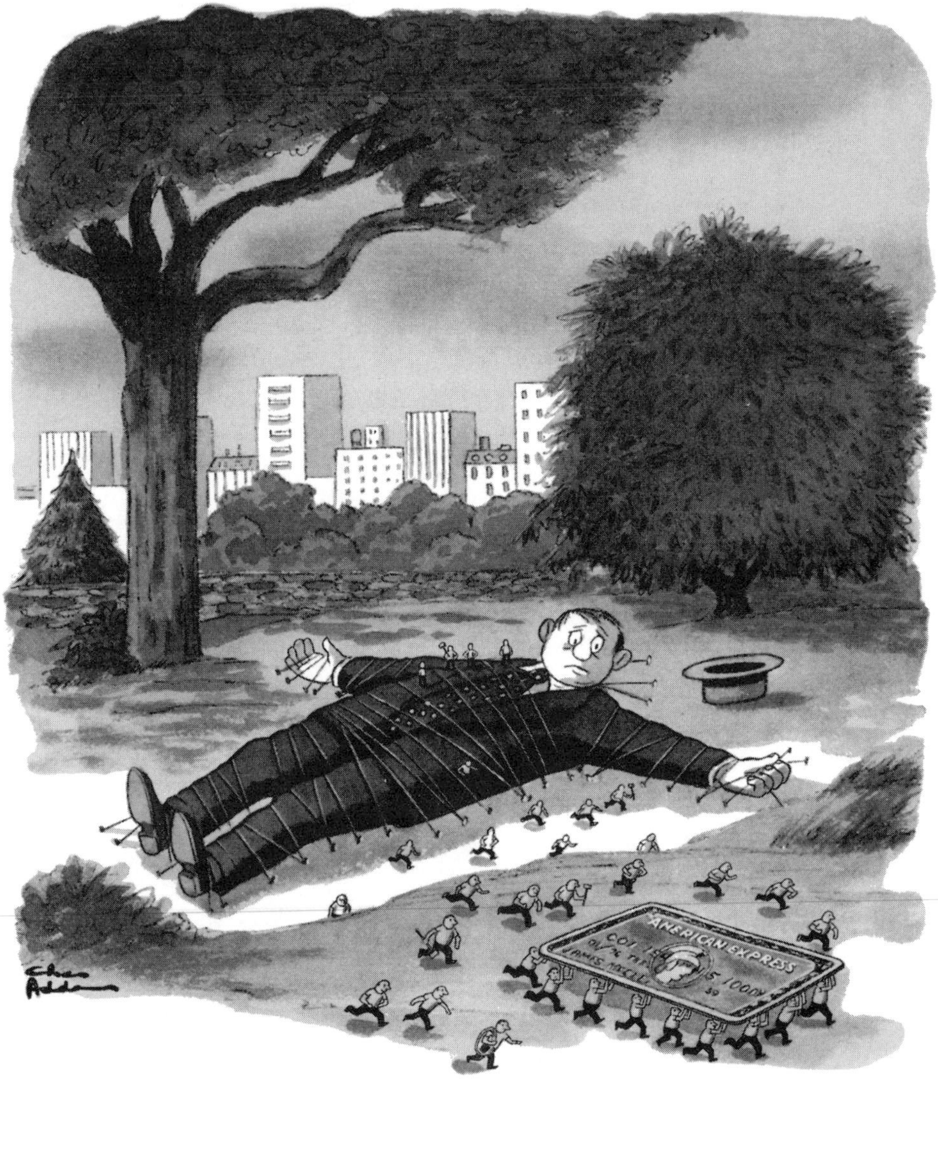
AMERICAN EXPRESS

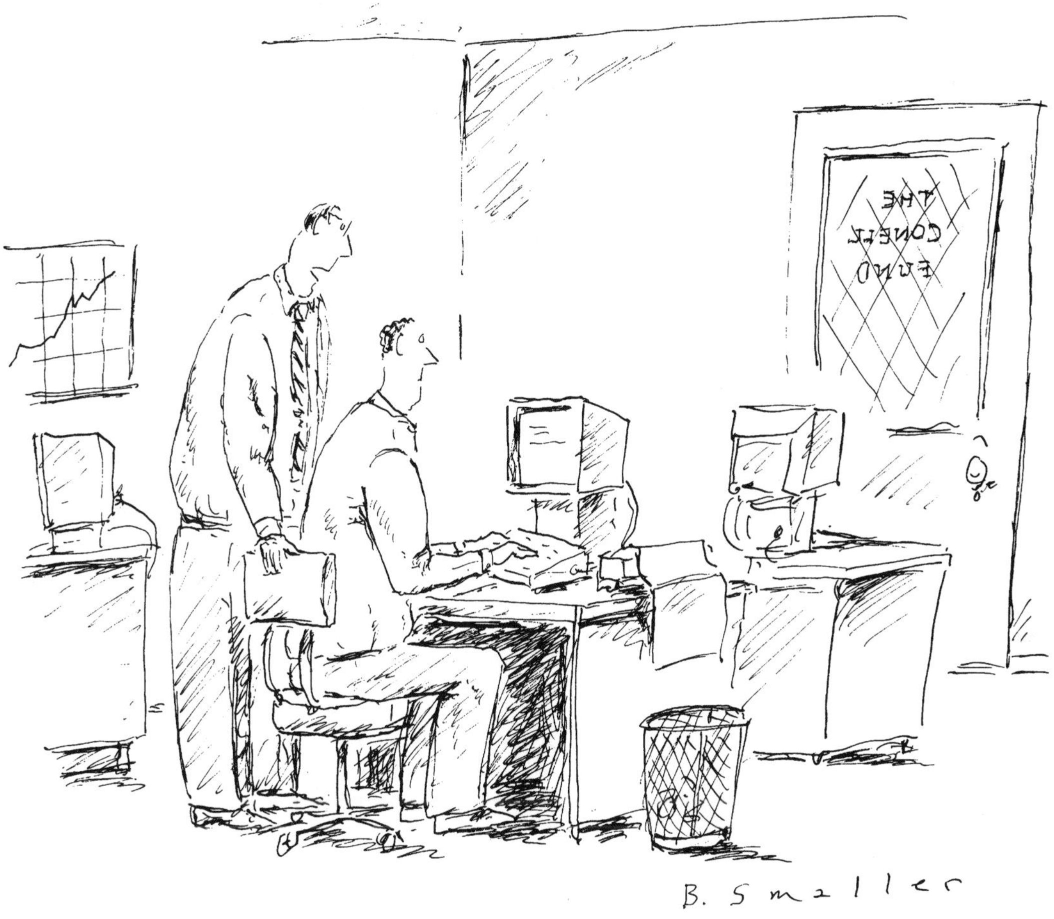
B. Smaller

"Up a hundred and sixteen points! If only we'd had the foresight to invest ten minutes ago."

"I thought I had the flu last weekend, but it was my hedge fund."

"Looks like broker-assisted suicide."

"*Three wishes less commission.*"

"*To relieve the pressure of your medical bills, I'm going to recommend that we go ahead and drain your savings account.*"

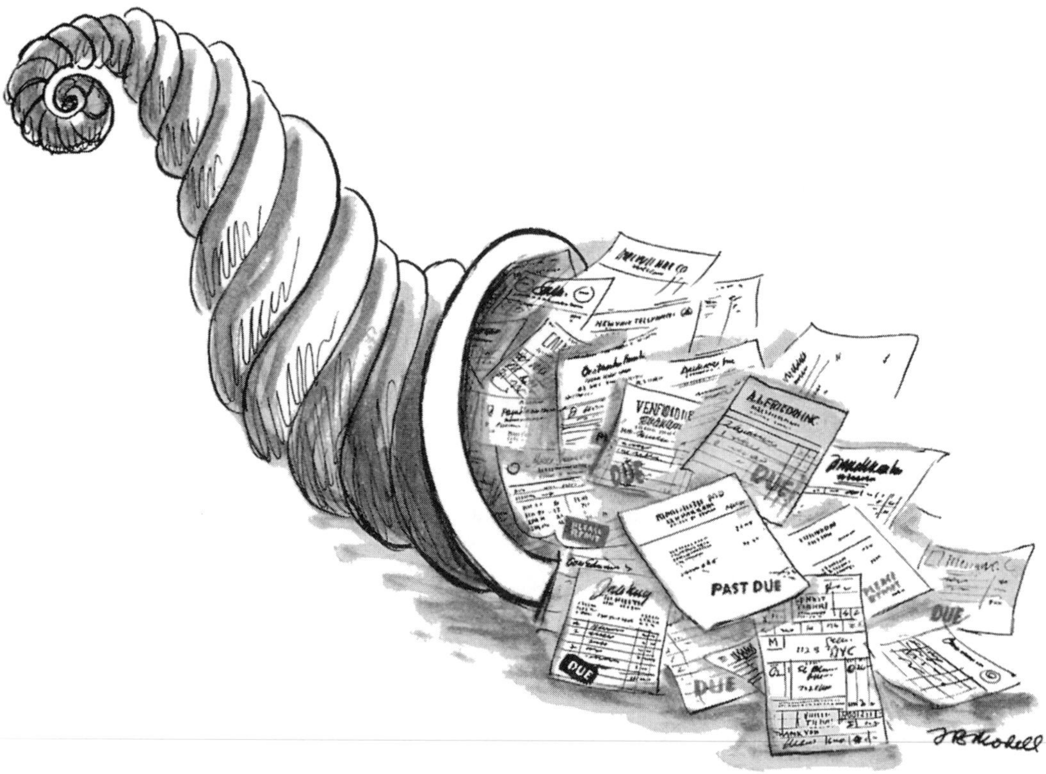
PAST DUE
DUE
DUE
DUE
DUE
DUE

"You may be in love, but can you support my daughter on what a herring makes?"

"Is there someone here who is sensitive to the banking needs of women?"

"*As a nation, we may be spending our children's money, but at my house it's the other way around.*"

VENUS
MERCURY
MARS
EARTH
JUPITER
SATURN
URANUS
NEPTUNE
PLUTO
THE CHECK
IN THE MAIL
ZIEGLER

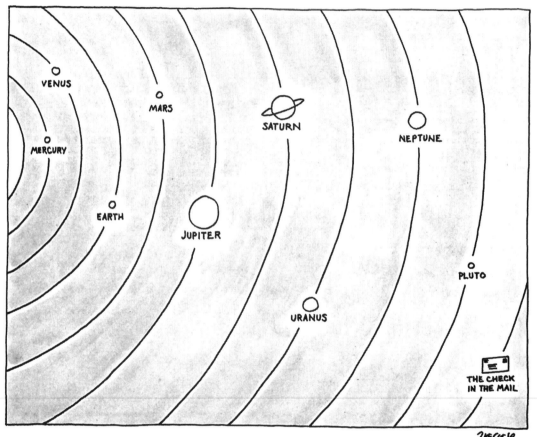

"We're pushing forty. Shouldn't we have a house, or something?"

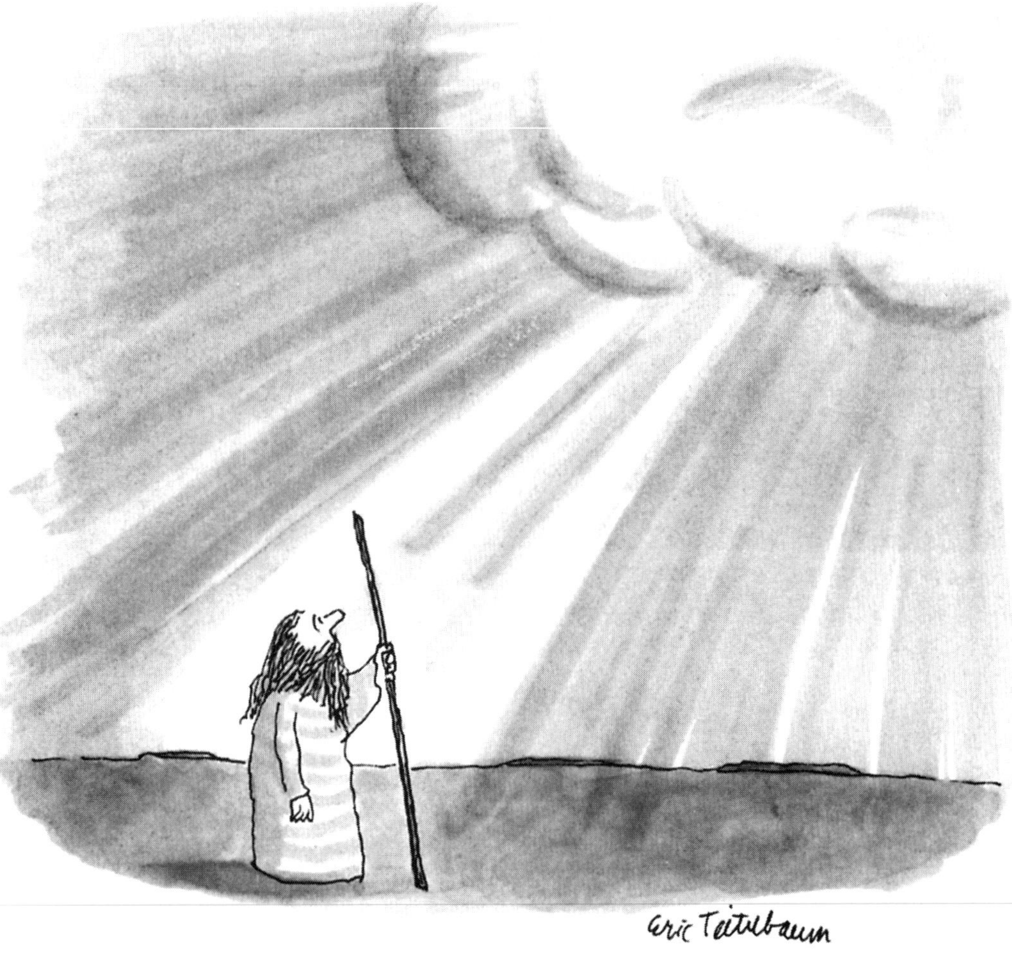
Eric Teitelbaum

"Now go forth as an independent contractor, keeping a careful diary of your travel expenses."

"*I hear Midas is putting everything into gold.*"

"It's true that more is not necessarily better, Edward, but it frequently is."

UNUSUAL RETIREMENT PLANS

1000-F.A.I.

I'll take a thousand bucks, stick it in a bank, "forget about it," and in thirty years I'll be _pleasantly surprised_.

M.K. Plan

"My Kids" will take care of me. I'm virtually certain of that.

Jackpot Account

I'm not going to need one, because I'm going to be _RICH_, yessirree Bob.

The ? Plan

Who can plan, like, _next week_? Because an asteroid could smash into the Earth tomorrow, so what's the point?

"*I like the big questions—but I'm more comfortable with money.*"

"Your signature, Your Majesty, as well as your driver's license and a major credit card."

"I'm making a bundle on Wall Street, but it's not what I really want.
What I really want is to make a bundle uptown."

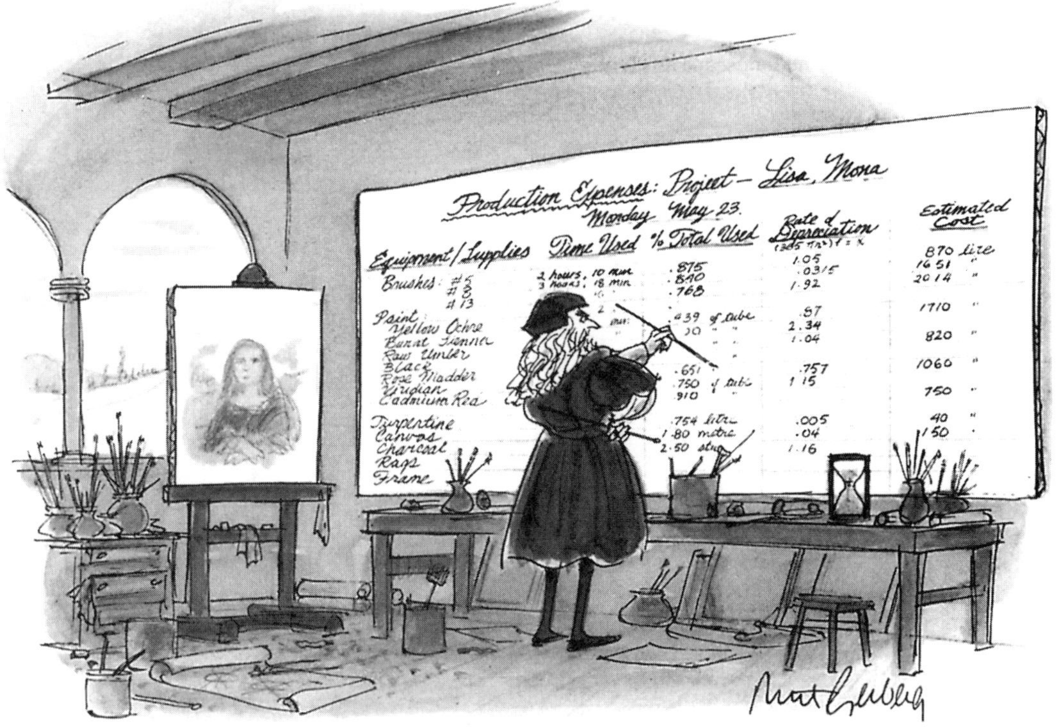

Production Expenses: Project — Lisa, Mona
Monday May 23.
Equipment / Supplies
Time Used
% Total Used
Rate of Depreciation
Estimated Cost
Brushes: #5
#8
#13
2 hours, 10 min
3 hours, 18 min
.875
.840
.768
1.05
.0315
1.92
870 lire
1651 "
2014 "
1710 "
Paint:
Yellow Ochre
Burnt Sienna
Raw Umber
Black
Rose Madder
Viridian
Cadmium Red
.439 of tube
.651
.750 of tube
.910
.87
2.34
1.04
.757
1.15
820 "
1060 "
750 "
Turpentine
Canvas
Charcoal
Rags
Frame
.754 litre
1.80 metre
.005
.04
1.16
40 "
150

LEONARDO MEETS THE I.R.S.

THE LAST OF THE MOM AND POP
BROKERAGE HOUSES

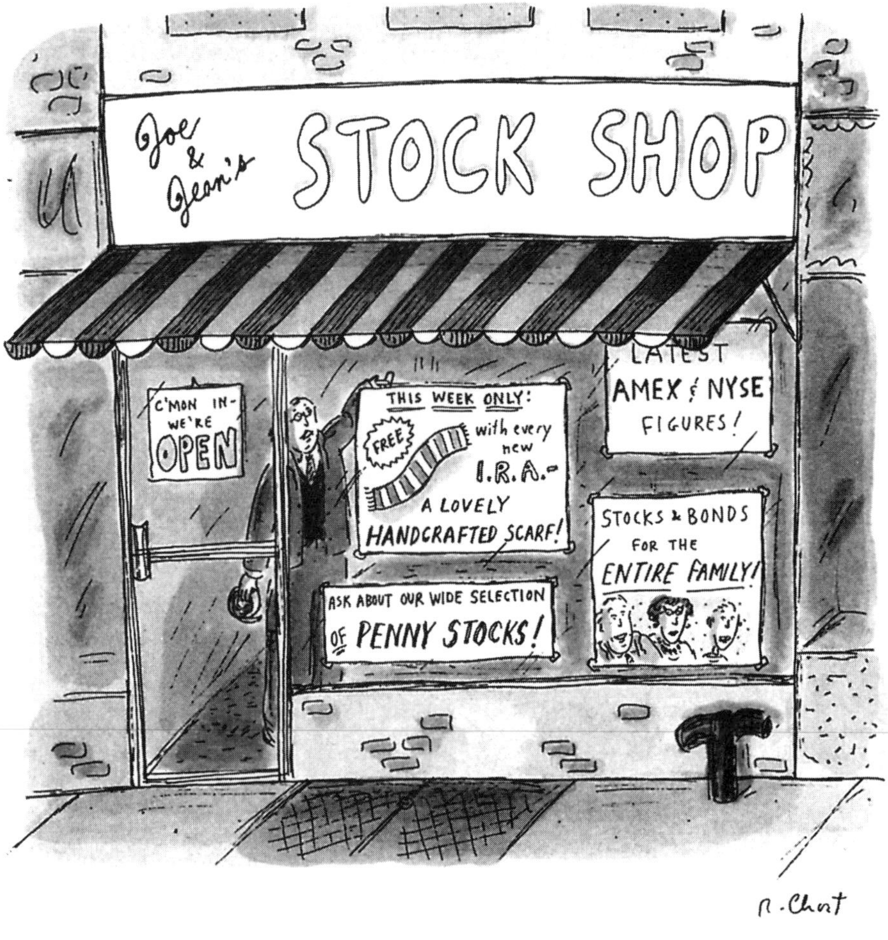

Joe & Jean's STOCK SHOP
C'MON IN- WE'RE OPEN
THIS WEEK ONLY: FREE with every new I.R.A.- A LOVELY HANDCRAFTED SCARF!
LATEST AMEX & NYSE FIGURES!
STOCKS & BONDS FOR THE ENTIRE FAMILY!
ASK ABOUT OUR WIDE SELECTION OF PENNY STOCKS!
R. Chast

"*You had more money than God. That's a big no-no.*"

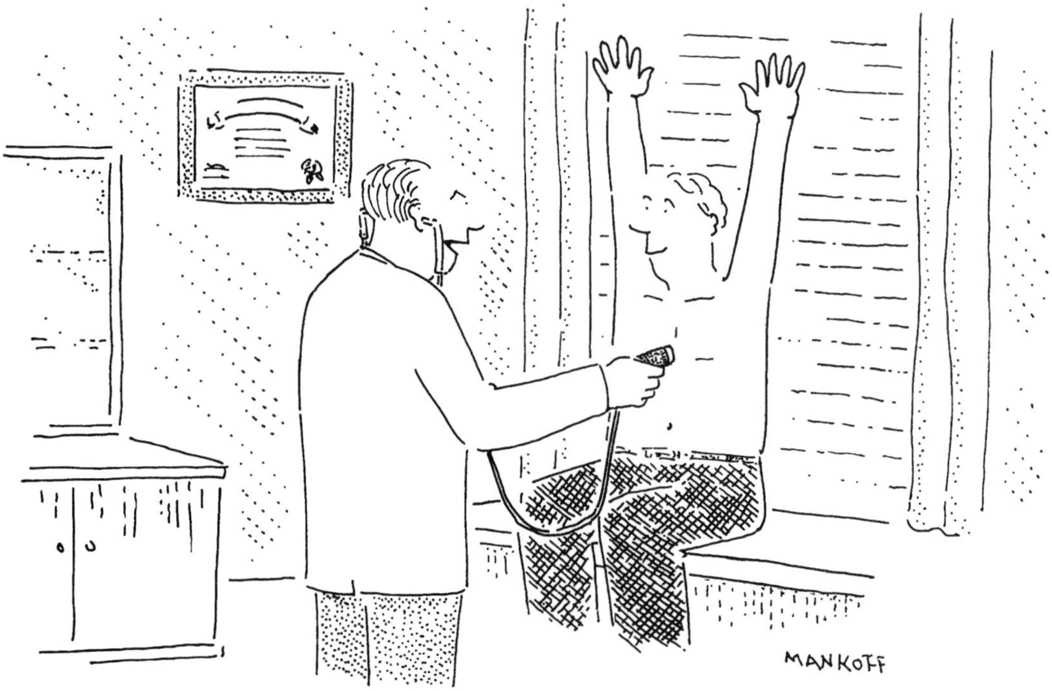
MANKOFF

"Very funny."

"*Will this be cash or consumer debt?*"

"Graduates, faculty, parents, creditors . . ."

"Winning is crucial to my retirement plans."

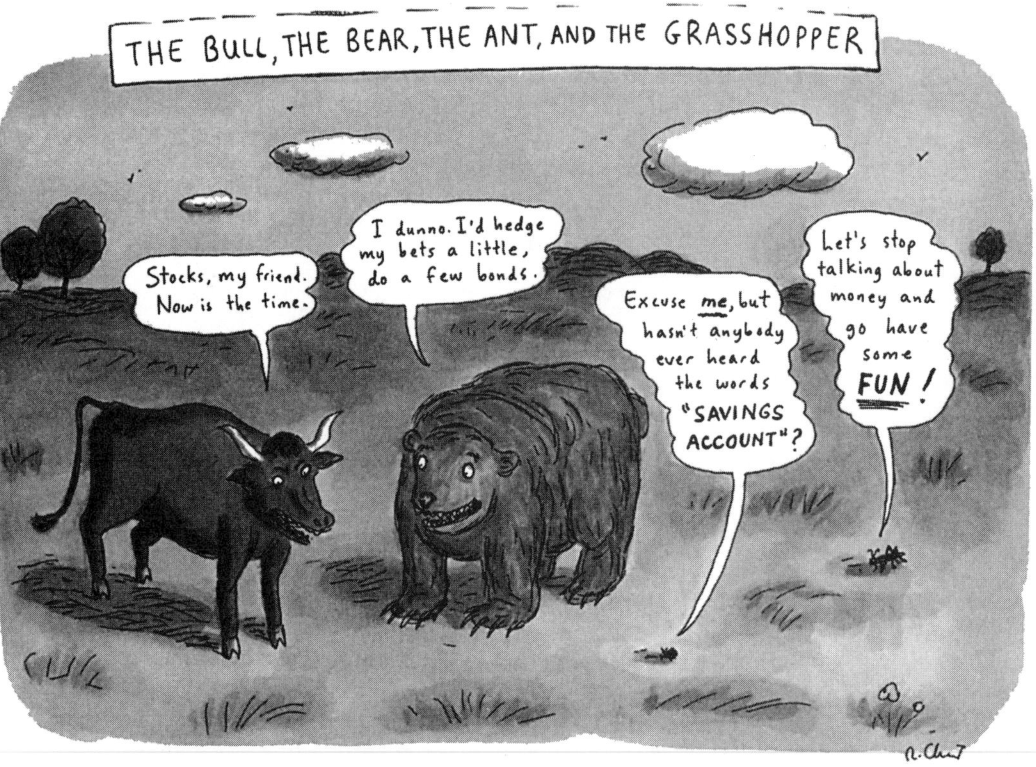
THE BULL, THE BEAR, THE ANT, AND THE GRASSHOPPER
Stocks, my friend. Now is the time.
I dunno. I'd hedge my bets a little, do a few bonds.
Excuse me, but hasn't anybody ever heard the words "SAVINGS ACCOUNT"?
Let's stop talking about money and go have some FUN!

"To wealth, even if it's only on paper."

"I'd love to, Barbara, but I'll have to check with the Bundesbank."

"His will reads as follows: 'Being of sound mind and disposition, I blew it all.'"

"Well, anyhow, it sure is handy having
my broker right here in my cell!"

"*Kids, your mother and I have spent so much money on health insurance this year that instead of vacation we're all going to go in for elective surgery.*"

"Oh, I'm really sorry. I just placed three million with
some broker who called five minutes ago."

"A collection agency is threatening air strikes."

"And just why do we always call <u>my</u> income the second income?"

ROLAINS. PLITOT
Born - 80 DOW
Died - 9,000 DOW

D. Reilly

"As far as I'm concerned, they can do what they want with the minimum wage, just as long as they keep their hands off the maximum wage."

"Love you, love us, and I'm comfortable with our debt level."

"So how's everything going?"

02732946 AL2
021193
PAY TO THE
ORDER OF
$ 1642.90
ORTY TWO DOLLARS AND
FIRST
BANK & TRUST
COMPTROLLER
0163302-7

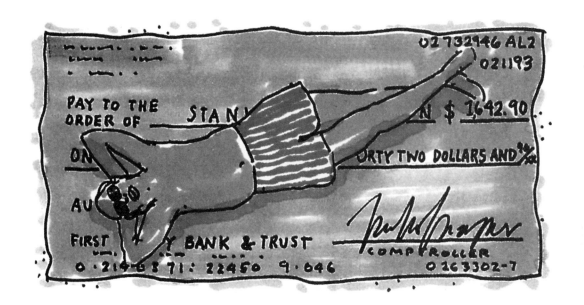

"I think globally, but I spend locally."

"Thanks for a wonderful evening. May I have the receipts
if you aren't going to use them?"

"Some people say you can't put a price on a wife's twenty-seven years of loyalty and devotion. They're wrong."

"*Must you tell us what our daily share of the national debt is every time we sit down to dinner?*"

"How come Jasper's mutual fund is up twelve percent and mine's only up eight?"

"Forty-seven years old and I'm still a small investor."

"And to think if I hadn't been home having dinner I might have missed this wonderful investment opportunity."

"*You can't be too rich or too thin, and we're not.*"

YOUR PIZZA DOLLAR
RENT
WAGES
EXTRA CHEESE
GAS
ELECTRICITY
PEPPERONI
TAXES
MUSHROOMS
INSURANCE
MStevens

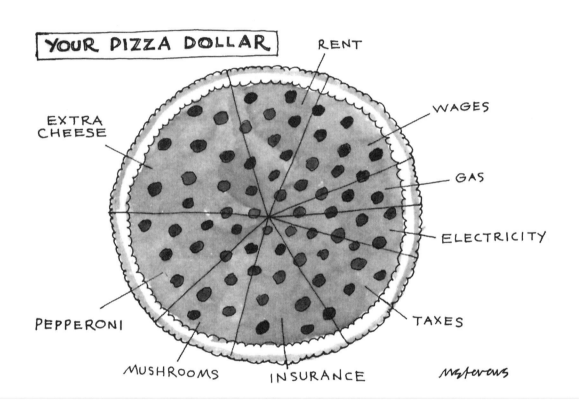

"Son, can you spare a couple of minutes to talk about your tuition?"

INTRODUCING...

THE 1040-F.I.* FORM

* THE TAX RETURN FOR THE FINANCIALLY INCOMPETENT

① How much money do you guess you made last year?

- ☐ Under $10,000.
- ☐ Somewhere between $10,000 and $100,000.
- ☐ More than $100,000, but I don't know how or why.

② Did you save any receipts?

- ☐ I tried, but I just couldn't.
- ☐ I think there're some in a shoebox. I'll go look.
- ☐ No. What am I, an <u>accountant</u>?

③ Check payment preference.

- ☐ How could I owe anything? My year was lousy.
- ☐ Here's $15,000. If you need more, let me know.
- ☐ Blank check enclosed. <u>You</u> fill it in. Whatever.

"Which Microsoft millionaire are you thinking about *now*?"

"My first Social Security check."

"*Your mother called to remind you to diversify.*"

"His final wish was that all his medical bills be paid promptly."

"Hi, I'm the tooth fairy. Want to buy back some of your teeth?"

"It's a check for a hundred thousand dollars. Do you like it?"

"A fantastic evangelist was on TV, and I sent him everything."

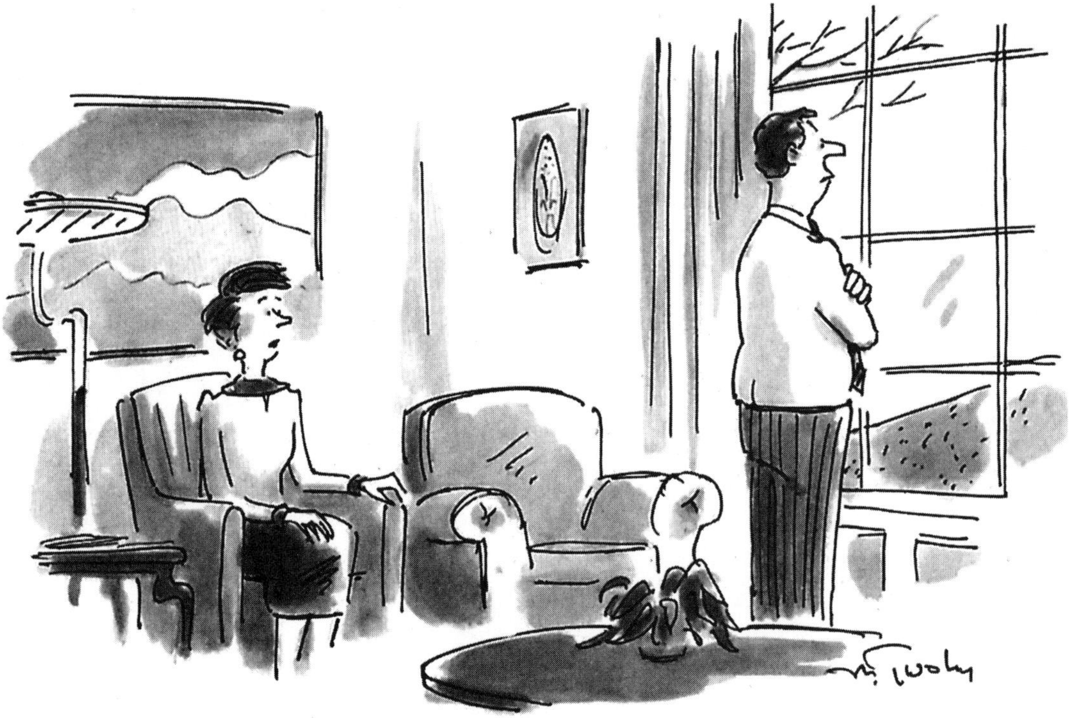
M. Twohy

"I'm sorry if my income is hurtful to you."

"And remember, son, perception isn't reality—money is."

"*Eventually I'd like to have a business where the money
rolls in and I wouldn't have to be there much.*"

"Dow Jonesy enough for you?"

"That's it. I'm taking the buyout."

"*Let's face it—man's best friend is money.*"

"Listen, Connie, Ronald and I are thinking about
getting married, and we were wondering if you could
get us some prices."

"My fees are quite high, and yet you say you have little money.
I think I'm seeing a conflict of interest here."

"We got a great buy on the apartment, but, unfortunately, it didn't include the mineral rights."

"Oh, by the way, do you have any money? Will you send me any money?
Do you know anyone who has any money? Will they send me any money?"

"*Of course they're clever. They have to be clever.*
They haven't got any money."

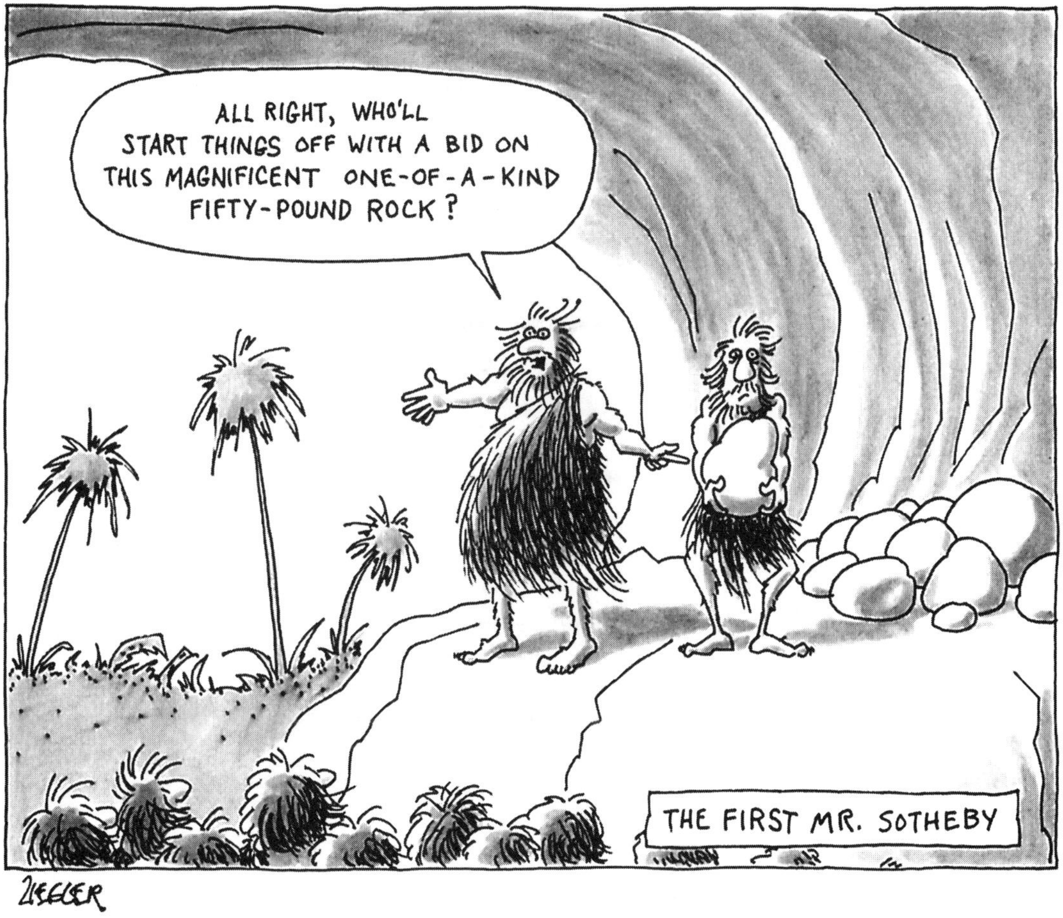
ALL RIGHT, WHO'LL START THINGS OFF WITH A BID ON THIS MAGNIFICENT ONE-OF-A-KIND FIFTY-POUND ROCK?
THE FIRST MR. SOTHEBY
ZIEGLER

"I wish I had the funding to really say something."

"I just figured it out—we're in the cheap seats."

"On the other hand, the examined life doesn't seem to produce much income."

"I'm afraid we'll need more time to fight for the check."

"*I don't suppose you remembered the tax-deduction forms that
I asked you to bring last year, did you?*"

"Dear Sir: You're probably asking yourself,
'Why do I need another credit card?'"

"New money, Bobby, is old money that got away."

"Fifty is plenty."

"Hundred and fifty."

"See? Isn't this better than being happy?"

"I just know I'm going to love horses all my life. That's why I'm planning to have a career in banking, insurance, and real estate."

"I'd like to bounce a check."

"*Broderick, promise you'll tell me if our living standard ever rises
at the expense of those less fortunate.*"

"Your money <u>was</u> working for you, but it suddenly quit and now it's working for me!"

SIZZLING BUCKS
EAVESDROP ON AMERICA'S LUSTIEST C.E.O.S AS THEY SHARE THEIR FANTASIES OF DOMINANCE + HUMILIATION
"I WAS SPANKED BY ALAN GREENSPAN."
"MORE!" THEY PLEADED, "MORE!"
"THOUSANDS WATCHED AS I WAS FORCED TO SUBMIT TO THE S.E.C."
DIAL 1-900 HOT CASH
(ADULTS ONLY)

"Hello. May I speak to my broker, please?"

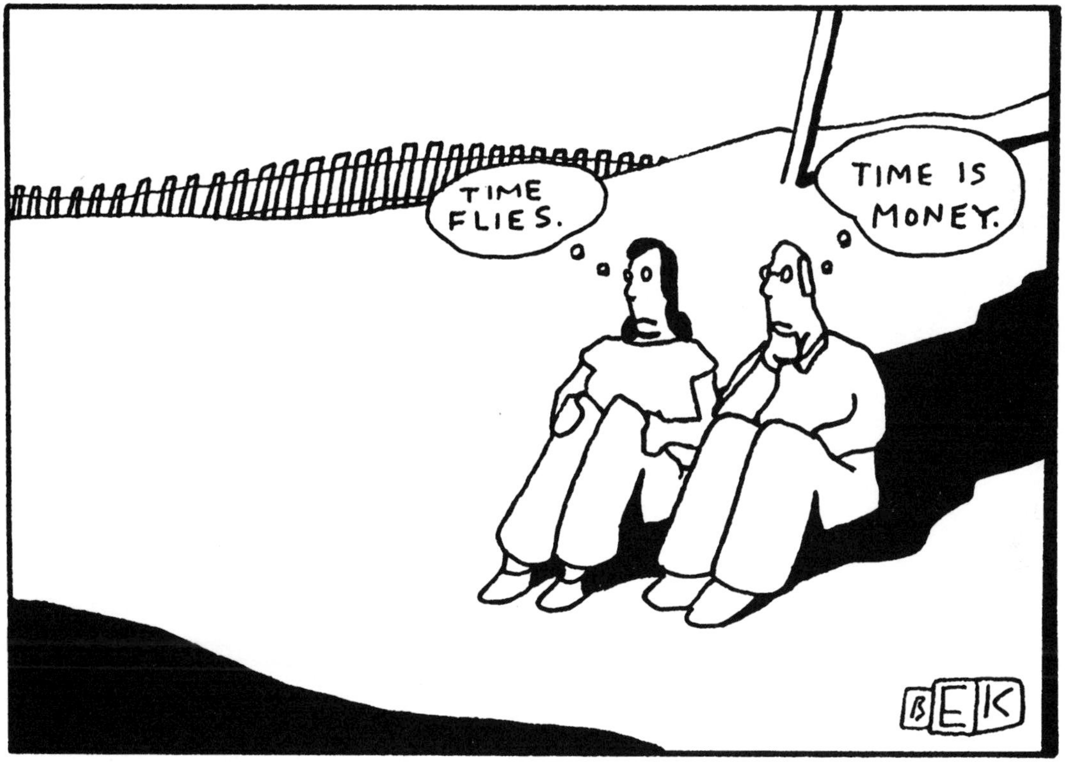
TIME FLIES.
TIME IS MONEY.
BEK

"*Dad, the dean has gone over your financial statement, and he doesn't think you're working up to your full potential.*"

"*Mrs. Beasley wants to borrow a cup of money.*"

It's time for **YOU** to start banking at the

FIRST NATIONAL ARTISTE SAVINGS & LOAN

Friendly tellers who will never, _ever_ laugh at you.

Special loans having nothing to do with real estate or cars.

Interesting, unbourgeois premiums.

Signed Dali lithograph (unframed)

Paperback of Walt Whitman's poems

Recently reissued Ornette Coleman record

Officers who understand your particular set of problems.

R. Chast

"To the rich, the very rich, and the super rich! Have I left anybody out?"

"Must you people always call at dinnertime?"

"Money doesn't trickle down unless there's a damn leak."

"One thing we do share with you—we both live on capital accumulated by others."

"Remember a few years ago when everything was sex, sex, sex?"

"I'm putting all my money into 'things.'"

"*There, there it is again—the invisible hand of the marketplace giving us the finger.*"

"*Gee, these new twenties look just like Monopoly money.*"

INDEX OF ARTISTS